THE STORY

BRADFORD

by

Alan Avery

BP

BLACKTHORN PRESS

Blackthorn Press, Blackthorn House
Middleton Rd, Pickering YO18 8AL
United Kingdom

ISBN 978 1 906259 07 5

www.blackthornpress.com

Book design by Simon Ellis
Email: simon@flexibubbleart.co.uk

CONTENTS

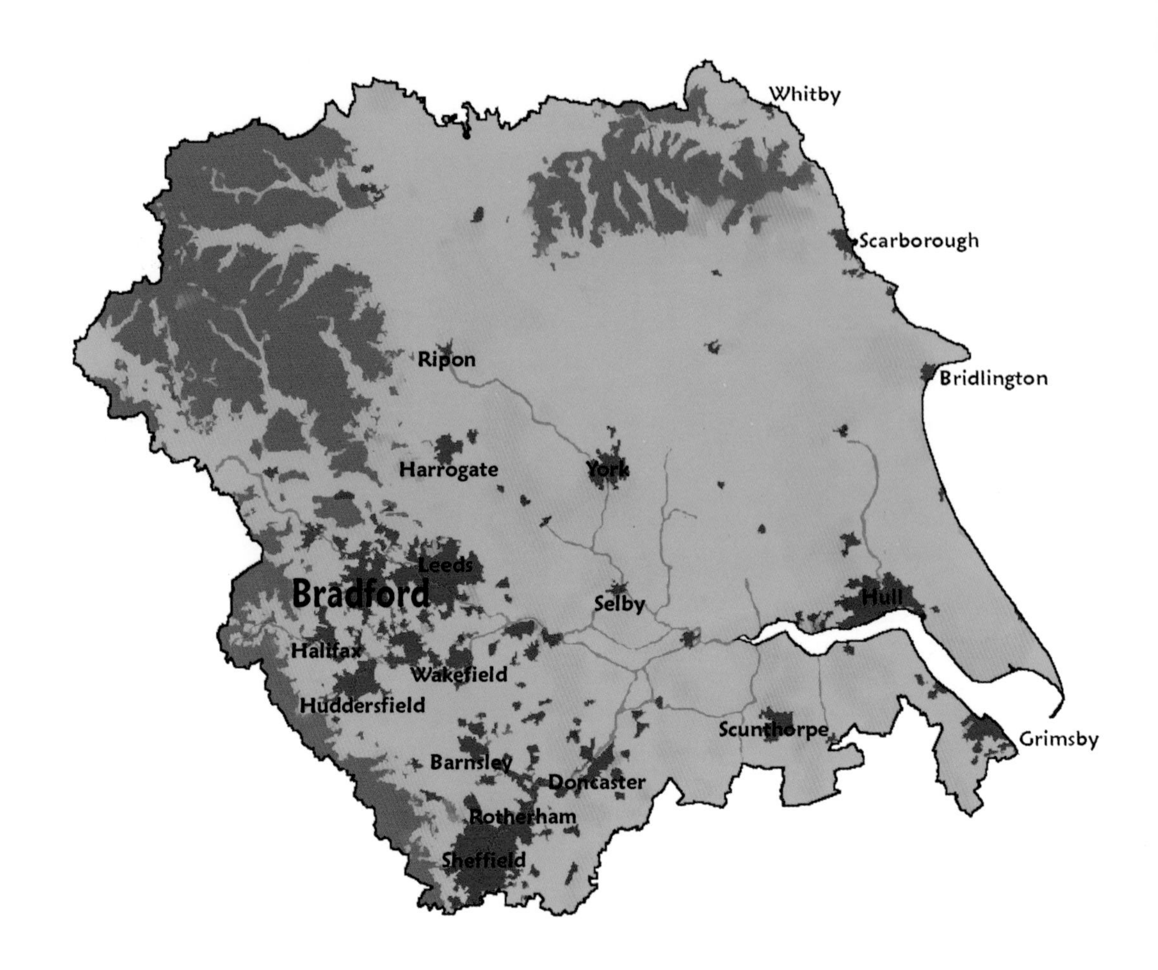

YORKSHIRE & HUMBERSIDE

THE BEGINNINGS OF BRADFORD

Today, Bradford is a city of some 310,000 inhabitants, its boundaries spreading out into the West Yorkshire countryside and merging with the neighbouring towns and cities into a vast conurbation of some two million people.

Yet the beginnings of the city are obscure and not until the eleventh century are written records available which cast some light onto the lives of the people who inhabited the same ground now walked on by the modern citizens. For a glimpse of these early lives we are dependent on the finds of the archaeologist.

Certainly, the area of Bradford Dale, where Bradford stands, is rich in archaeological finds of stone axes and flints. These ranged from the earliest hunters who roamed the wooded valleys about ten thousand years ago, tracking game and gathering wild fruits, to the more settled farmers who reared cattle and cleared and cultivated the land and made pottery, wove cloth and used bronze tools and weapons. The unexplained cup and ring markings, carved into the local stone, can be found all over the world but are concentrated in Britain in the area around Bradford and probably date from some four thousand years ago. By the iron age of two thousand years ago, we know the area was inhabited by the Celtic tribe called the Brigantes and it may be that Bradford's position at the ford of the Bradford Beck meant that there was some kind of settlement or village inhabited by the Brigantes, although this is pure speculation. However, the Celtic carved stone heads which can be seen at Cartwright Hall are found more abundantly in this area than anywhere else in Britain, suggesting that the area was of some importance in pre-Roman times.

Above
Cup and ring markings

Left
Celtic Stone Head

The Romans arrived in Yorkshire in 71 AD and set up their Legionary fort at York. From there, a network of roads and minor forts spread out to subdue the local tribes and facilitate trade. The nearest Roman fort to Bradford was at Ilkley, some twelve miles away to the north and the road from York to Manchester probably ran by modern Bradford but despite finds of Roman coins, some evidence of iron working and the suggestion that Tong Street is of Roman origin, there is no evidence of any Roman occupation in the immediate area of Bradford.

When the Romans left Britain in 410 AD they were quickly followed by Anglo-Saxon raiders from Germany who then came to settle more permanently. We can trace the spread of the largely Anglian tribes through East and North Yorkshire by tracing their place names and tracking their burial sites, which contained distinctive pottery and other artefacts. They were in York by 490 but the Anglian settlement of West Yorkshire was delayed by the resistance of the Celtic Kingdom of Elmet, which was largely based in the West Riding and was well enough organised and led to hold back the tide until 616, when it was defeated and absorbed by the Anglian King Edwin. Today the Celtic Kingdom is remembered in such place names as Sherburn in Elmet.

Right
The Celts ruled West Yorkshire

Again, we can trace the spread of the Anglian tribesmen into the West Riding by place names, archaeological finds and DNA evidence. The popular image is one of Anglian warriors slaughtering the native Celts, taking over their land and driving them ever westwards. There may well be some truth in this but recent DNA evidence suggests that the Celts were as much absorbed into Anglian society as driven out. Whatever the pattern of conquest may have been, the Angles settled in and around Bradford and gave it its modern name, meaning 'broad ford' in Old English. There was a small settlement around the ford of Bradford Beck in the centre of the modern city and we can surmise that it, in its turn, was taken over by the Viking raiders of the ninth century although evidence for Scandinavian settlement in the area is scarce. It is not until the making of the Domesday Book in 1086 when the new king, William I, sent out commissioners to take an inventory of his newly conquered land that Bradford steps out of conjecture and imagination into recorded history.

Left
The Anglians built the first settlement and gave Bradford its name

BRADFORD IN THE MIDDLE AGES

The record for Bradford in the Domesday book is terse but tells us that the small village and the land around it belonged to Gamel, who was presumably of Scandinavian origin, and that before the Norman Conquest he owned 1,500 acres of land worth £4 but that now the land was 'waste'. This sudden fall in the value of Bradford and the land around it is was owing to the actions of King William who in revenge for an uprising in Yorkshire against his rule burned and pillaged vast tracks of the county. The population of Bradford at this time was probably no more than 250. There was a wooden hall, where the lord lived and possibly a small chapel. The few villagers' houses were clustered around the hall. Bees were kept for wax and honey and there was fishing in the becks and rivers. The villagers ground their corn by hand and kept pigs in the village and sheep on the surrounding hills.

Below
Bradford's entry in the Doomsday Book

M In BRADEFORD cu vi. bereuuit. hb Gamel. xv.
car tre ad gld. ubi poss. ee. viij. car. Ilbt ht. 7 Wast
est. T.R.E. ual. iiij. lib. Silua past dim leu lg. 7 di
lat.

William rewarded the knights who had followed him from Normandy and fought at Hastings with vast tracts of land and Bradford was awarded to the de Lacy family who had their main residence at Pontefract castle and probably only visited Bradford and the other parts of their estates on rare occasions when travelling or hunting.

Right
Ilbert de Lacy was awarded Bradford by William I

With the twists and turns of fortune, the village of Bradford changed hands many times in the Middle Ages as magnates fell in and out of favour with the monarch. These changes of ownership often meant an inventory or 'inquisition' of Bradford and these offer a remarkable set of documents, which mark the development of the small settlement. We know that in 1281 Alice de Lacy gave ninety-six acres of land to the church in Bradford and that the priest at that time was Robert Tonnington. The Lord of Bradford also held a court in the village, where instant justice was dispensed and fines gathered in. An interesting entry in an early record of court fines mentions 'Evam, the weaver' indicating that weaving was already taking place in Bradford from early in the Middle Ages.

Above There were Weavers in Bradford early in the Middle Ages

The de Lacys kept Bradford until 1310 and in their time the nearby Kirstall Abbey was founded and, more importantly for Bradford, Edmund de Lacy obtained permission from Henry III to hold a weekly market in 1251 and in 1294 Henry de Lacy obtained a charter from the king allowing him to hold an annual fair. Markets and fairs were of vital importance to the economy of the Middle Ages for here produce from the countryside could be bought or exchanged for such goods as the town could produce. The market at Bradford was held in the churchyard until well into the sixteenth century. The Inquisition of 1311, held on the death of Henry de Lacy, details the manor house, at this time rebuilt in stone and a water mill and a fulling mill, again indicating that cloth was an important part of the village's economy. We also know that by 1379 there were twenty-eight houses, as well as the simple crofts of the labourers and three inns, all huddled round Kirkgate, Westgate and Ivegate. The population by 1400 has been estimated at 700 people.

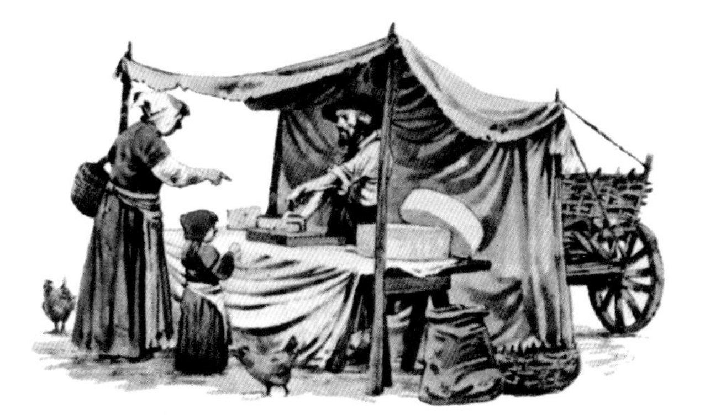

Left A market was held in Bradford from 1251

Above
Bradford was reduced to poverty by the Black Death

Despite this early growth, progress was neither uniform nor continuous. Bradford was raided by the Scots and the church almost completely destroyed. Worse was to come in 1349 when the Black Death arrived in the town and the population was reduced to less than one hundred adults living in poverty. Bradford was part of the Duchy of Lancaster and men from Bradford took up arms for the red rose in the Wars of the Roses and presumably many lost their lives at the decisive battle of Towton in 1461, which took place only twenty miles from Bradford. Yet by the end of the Middle Ages in 1485, there was some recovery. The church was slowly being rebuilt and improved, although the tower was not finished until 1508 and a new chapel dedicated to St Sitha was built at the end of the Ivebridge. By 1500 the new manor hall in Kirkgate was completed. Cloth making was the main trade but shoe making and tanning were also carried out in the town and the shoemakers of Bradford are mentioned in an Elizabethan play;

I think we are now in Bradford,
Where all the merry shoemakers dwell.

Certainly, the tanners were being fined at the court for polluting the beck with their sweepings. In 1461 trade in the town was strong enough to warrant the granting of a second annual fair to which traders in wool and leather would come from around the county to buy and barter.

Legend of the boar

Bradford's coat-of-arms displays a boar with no tongue and three hunting horns. This unusual emblem stems from a Medieval story about a fierce boar which was terrorising the neighbourhood of Bradford. The king offered a reward for anyone who would kill it and when a huntsman called John Northrop, came across the boar at a drinking hole, he quickly fired an arrow and dispatched it and then cut out its tongue as proof of his deed and set off to find the king to claim his prize. Meanwhile another man came across the body of the boar and cut off its head and likewise set off to claim the reward. He arrived at court first, showed the head and asked for his reward. However, someone pointed out that the boar had no tongue and the man was unable to explain why. Northrop arrived shortly afterwards with the tongue and all was made clear. He was awarded a parcel of land on the condition that he blew a horn three times at Bradford Market on St Martin's day.

TUDOR BRADFORD

When Henry Tudor was victorious over Richard III at the battle of Bosworth in 1485 and began the Tudor family's long occupation of the English throne, he started a period of national growth and prosperity which culminated in the reign of Elizabeth I. Bradford was to enjoy the fruits of this prosperity with increasing growth and wealth.

National concerns were not to impinge on Bradford until the reign of Henry VIII, which began in 1509. In need of money to fight his wars and a divorce from his first wife to secure a male heir to the throne, Henry turned his attention to the wealth of the church. He began by confiscating smaller religious houses and then the larger.

Right
Henry VIII

Closures of monasteries and nunneries took place all over the country as Henry's need for money, mixed with the new ideas of the Reformation, to bring about mass confiscations of church property and brutality against any who dared to voice opposition to the reforms. No one was safe, from Thomas More the chancellor who was executed in 1535 to humble friars who were burned for refusing to accept the king's authority. Bradford lost the nearby Cistercian priory of Esholt in 1536 where the few remaining nuns were pensioned off.

The backlash against these changes came in the north of England and was known as the 'Pilgrimage of Grace'. Under their leader, Robert Aske, a huge army of 40,000 men backed by leading northern aristocrats, like the Percys, demanded the restoration of the monasteries and the end of reform. Sir Richard Tempest of Bradford's Bolling Hall joined in the rebellion. Faced with so large a rebellion, Henry backed down, promising the Pilgrims all they asked at a meeting in Doncaster but once they had dispersed he moved quickly to round up and execute the leaders and a proportion of the population of every town and village involved. Sir Richard Tempest died in prison in 1537. Others, such as Walter Paslew, who had bought up land which had belonged to the monks of Rievaulx, had done well out of the dissolutions and were natural supporters of Henry. Land had become generally more widely owned, creating a class of independent yeomen farmers, free from medieval ties and not to be dominated by the parson or the squire.

Below
The Duke of Norfolk turns back the Pilgrimage of Grace

Above
Elizabeth I

Elizabeth I never visited Yorkshire but her religious reforms were felt in Bradford as elsewhere in the county. Following the death of Henry VIII the country had swung first back to Catholicism under his daughter, Mary and then back to an extreme form of Protestantism under his son, Edward. Henry's last child, Elizabeth, attempted to bring in a form of national religion which, if not tolerant, at least avoided the worst extremes of earlier times. Like much of the West Riding, Bradford adopted the Puritan form of Anglicanism which suited their independent spirit and their beliefs in hard work and its just rewards.

Despite recurrences of the plague in the sixteenth century, the population of Bradford had reached an estimated 2,500 by 1602. The medieval wooden houses had been largely replaced by two storey stone dwellings, Bolling Hall being the most prominent restructured building, and there was a grammar school. Farming alone was unable to support this growing population and with the low start up costs required, many turned to the textile industry as a means of earning a living. In 1536 John Leland had visited Bradford and noted that 'It standith much by clothing' and this association with Bradford and the clothing trade was to grow markedly in the next century.

Above
Bolling Hall

William Bull

William Bull is typical of the independent craftsmen of Bradford who were prepared to stand up for what they thought rather than believe what was expected of them. In 1543 he was taken before the Archbishop's court at York accused of heresy. In his defence he said that he would rather be confessed by a layman than by a priest unless the priest could show him such words as he would ask of him from the Epistle and the Gospels. And he certainly wouldn't confess to a priest, especially if he had seduced a fair woman as the priest would be chasing after her himself in a few days.

STUART BRADFORD

The weaving of woollen cloth had become Bradford's chief industry in the seventeenth century. By 1612 it has been estimated that some 20,000 people were working in the cloth-making industry in Bradford and Halifax.

Many of these workers were also farmers who were unable to make a living on the small acreage many of them held and turned to weaving to supplement the family income. Indeed, cloth making was a family affair. A farmer might install a loom in one of his rooms and buy in the wool from a local farmer. The wool would be spun by his unmarried daughters (hence our word 'spinster') or sent out to local women and then woven by himself or one of his sons. The cloth would be taken to the local fulling mill for finishing and the cloth piece then taken to Bradford market for sale to visiting merchants from London or exported via York and Hull.

Right
Cloth was woven at home

Much cloth was produced on this small scale but a landowner with the capital behind him could own several looms and hire dozens of women with spinning wheels to feed the looms. At this stage, only the fulling mills with their water driven hammers were anything like mechanised. Cloth manufacture was very much a hand and home industry.

Bradford was increasingly growing beyond its original core of houses clustered around the beck. To the east of the beck was the church, grammar school and farmlands whereas the west side of the town was the commercial heart where the market, court and manor house were situated.

Bradford's steady growth was interrupted by the Civil War which was to cause much damage and suffering to Bradford. Relations between King Charles I and his Parliament in London deteriorated to such an extent that Charles fled the capital in March 1642 and moved his family and court to York making it, in effect, the capital of England. The king left York on the 16 August for Nottingham leaving a garrison of 4,000 soldiers under the Duke of Newcastle. At Nottingham the king raised his standard, declaring the opening of hostilities between himself and Parliament and the beginning of the Civil War, which would only end with the king's execution in 1649.

Left Charles I

Sentiment in Bradford was overwhelmingly for Parliament. The population was largely Puritan whereas the King had a Catholic wife and was rumoured to be a Catholic himself. Moreover, in his desperate need for money, Charles had sold off the manor of Bradford and placed a high church vicar in the church and a papist sympathiser as headmaster of the school. And it was the Catholic Tempest family who tried to bring back old feudal laws and taxes for the benefit of London financiers. Worst of all, the crown tried to enforce its old rights to tax cloth on its way to Hull and York for export and three years before the outbreak of the civil war Charles quartered troops in Bradford who made themselves thoroughly unpopular with their threatening behaviour.

When war finally broke out, Bradford was in a dangerous position. Royalist troops had left the town but Leeds, York and Wakefield were garrisoned. Bradford had no regular troops and few arms. The first attack came on the 23rd of October 1642 but the force of eight hundred irregular Royalist soldiers were easily repulsed by Bradford's 'Dad's Army'. The Royalists came back in December this time with cannon and eight hundred regular soldiers. Bradford could only muster 300 poorly armed men but snipers in the church tower killed many of the attackers. A blizzard blew up and an attack on the town was repulsed so that by the end of the day the Royalist army lost any spirit for the fight and made its way back to Leeds.

Above
The Third seige of Bradford

The Royalist forces returned on December 18th under the command of Captain Goodrich. Bradford's defenders had hung bales of wool on the church tower to defend it from cannon shot and after some fierce exchanges the day was saved for Bradford when reinforcements arrived from Bingley and Halifax and the Royalist army was again driven back to Leeds.

Lord Newcastle's
bed at Bolling Hall

The citizens of Bradford must have been relieved when Sir Thomas Fairfax arrived in the town with his regular troops in January 1643. Fairfax drove the Royalists out of Wakefield, Leeds and Pontefract and then commanded West Yorkshire and its trade until the summer of that year. On the 30th June the Royalist commander, the Earl of Newcastle himself, arrived with an army of 10,000 men and Fairfax took his force of 3,000 out of Bradford and met the Royalists on Adwalton Moor five miles south-west of Bradford. Despite the differences in number, the outcome of the battle was by no means certain until Fairfax took his cavalry off the battle field in pursuit of the Royalist cavalry and a charge of Royalist mounted pikemen, led by Colonel Skirton broke the left flank of the Parliamentarian army and the battle was over. Fairfax escaped to Hull and the remnants of his army trudged back to Bradford. The town was quickly surrounded by Newcastle's troops and realising the hopelessness of their position, the Parliamentarian troops escaped during the night leaving Bradford to its fate.

Lord Newcastle had taken over Bolling Hall and there is a local legend that a ghostly figure of a lady appeared to him asking him to 'Pity Poor Bradford'. True or not, nobody in Bradford was harmed when the Royalist troops moved in, although they thoroughly sacked and looted the town. As if that were not bad enough, bubonic plague returned to the town in 1645 and again in 1665 and it can be seen from the parish register that the number of baptisms and marriages fell by a half up to 1659. The town's cause was not helped when a number of its leading citizens took part in a plot against the new King, Charles II, the so called Farnley Wood Plot, which ended in failure but gained Bradford a reputation for disloyalty.

Right
Bubonic plague came to Bradford in 1645

The parish church served the members of the Church of England although the character of the services would have changed depending whether the vicar was high or low church and there was an instance in 1672 when a vicar was ejected but continued to hold independent services in Horton Hall library. Quakers had been meeting since 1650. Their founder, George Fox, visited the town in 1652 and Quakers were to grow in number and influence throughout the century. Presbyterians had a 'preaching house' at Little Horton in 1688. However, there was still medieval superstition in men's minds and in 1650 a Bradford woman was tried at York Assizes for witchcraft.

Left
George Fox

Recovery was slow in the remainder of the seventeenth century. The fact that Parliament had to pass a law in 1666 declaring that all dead persons must be buried in wool clothing was an indication of the depressed state of woollen manufacture and the citizens of Bradford petitioned Parliament in 1687 to stop the manufacture of cane-bottomed chairs which had reduced the demand for the cloth they had previously been covered in but Parliament declined to act. There were, however, some signs of improvement in transport and communications but perhaps the most important change for the town was the switch from woollen cloth manufacture to worsted, a finer type of cloth, which would have important consequences in the next century.

Thomas Fairfax

Thomas Fairfax was born in Denton in Yorkshire in 1612. At the age of seventeen he was in Holland learning to be a soldier and at the outbreak of the civil war his skills were put at the service of Parliament. He served in campaigns throughout Yorkshire, especially in Bradford and Hull. He was made General of the Parliamentary cavalry and served with distinction at the battles of Marston Moor and Naseby. In 1650 he was ordered to march against the Scots who had declared Charles II king but he refused and retired into private life. With the death of Cromwell he was head of the commission sent to The Hague in 1660 to arrange for the return of Charles II. He died in 1671.

BRADFORD IN THE EIGHTEENTH CENTURY

For most of the eighteenth century Bradford remained a small manufacturing town, its population slowly increasing. The population at the beginning of the century was probably no more than 4,000 and this had grown to only 6,393 persons in the first national census of 1801. The phenomenal growth in population was not to happen until the following century.

Above
First known image of Bradford sketched in 1718

Progress was evident if slow. Bradford had its first postmaster in 1705 as the town was linked to the national postal service and in 1744 the first waterworks company opened a reservoir at the top of Westgate which held 15,000 gallons. The reservoir supplied stand pipes in Westgate, Ivegate, Kirkgate and Darley Street and it would be many years before water was piped into individual houses but it was a start. There was sufficient poverty amongst the population to warrant the building in 1738 of Bradford's first workhouse where the poor could be housed and fed and put to work. It lasted until 1851 when it was superseded by a larger workhouse built by the new Poor-Law institution. Crime and poverty continued to worry the respectable middle classes and in 1759 sixty of Bradford's inhabitants signed an undertaking to share the cost of bringing to justice any of the many burglars who appear to have been plaguing the town.

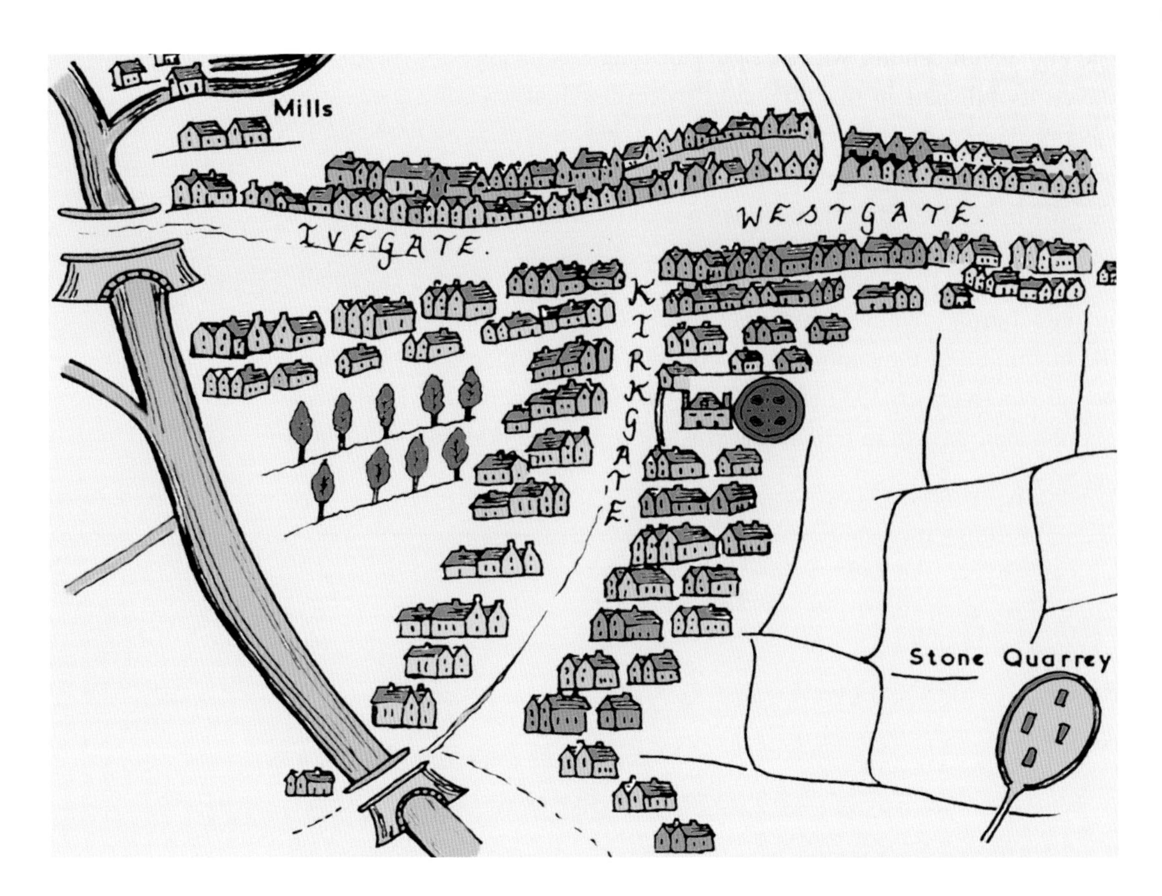

Above
Bradford 1722

The growing wealth of the worsted manufacturers and the general increase in trade warranted the building of the first 'Piece Hall' in 1773 where manufacturers could show and sell their finished products. The first Bradford bank opened in 1760, able to supply capital to those wanting to invest in new machines and to issue notes. The 'Worsted Committee' was established in 1777 to oversee any fraudulent practises in the manufacture of the cloth.

Working people were becoming sufficiently organised and politicised for Parliament to pass an Act in 1726, forbidding all combinations of woolcombers or weavers who were attempting to improve their conditions of labour and pay. In total defiance of this Act, a 'National Union of Hand Woolcombers' was formed in 1726, calling itself a 'sick club' to avoid the law and demanding that nobody should employ a weaver who was not a member of the club.

The eighteenth century was a century of religious change and Bradford played its full part in this change. Bradford's Quakers built their own Meeting House in 1698 but moved to a new, larger building in 1732. Baptists and Congregationalists had their own chapels by 1720 but it is the growth of Methodism in the town which was the most noticeable. The founder of Methodism, John Wesley, had met with John Nelson a stonemason of Bradford and inspired him to become the first Methodist preacher in Bradford. Nelson was seized by the press gang to be a soldier and was thrown into Bradford gaol, then situated at the junction of Kirkgate and Ivegate. Nelson was made of stern stuff and spent the night preaching to the crowd who had gathered outside and who supported him by singing hymns. Wesley was soon back in Bradford and his preaching to the working men and women drew large crowds and many were inspired to join the Methodist movement, the first Wesleyan 'society' being formed in 1749. There can be little doubt that the Methodist movement struck a chord with Bradford's working population. It preached in the streets rather than in the church and Meeting House, which were increasingly seen as only for the Middle Classes. By the middle of the next century of the 159 places of worship in Bradford, 79 were one of the various branches of Methodism. There was sufficient support for Methodism as early as 1767 for a permanent preacher's house to be built besides the newly opened Octagonal Chapel. Catholics, who had virtually disappeared in the 16th century returned to the town in 1753.

Below
John Wesley preached in the open air

Despite these many developments, it is the changes in Bradford's cloth manufacturing industries which are of most importance to the future of the town. Changes were to begin towards the end of the eighteenth century which were to alter the town beyond all recognition in the nineteenth.

A steady increase in the size and prosperity of the population of the UK and the increases in purchases of cloth from overseas meant that the demand for cloth rose steadily throughout the eighteenth century and then very rapidly in the nineteenth. The old system of hand spinning and weaving, the so-called 'putting out' system, was unable to cope with the demand and a series of inventions at the end of the eighteenth century gradually mechanised all aspects of the cloth industry. As early as 1733 Richard Kay invented a 'flying shuttle' which greatly increased the productivity of the weaver but put great pressure on the hand spinners to supply the spun thread. This discrepancy was overcome by the invention of Arkwright's 'Spinning Jenny' which could produce large quantities of thread by the turning of a wheel. The first 'Jenny' appeared in Bradford in 1765. By 1785 the mechanisation of the cloth making process was complete with the introduction of Cartwright's power loom. This process of industrialisation met with resistance from the workers who saw their skilled and relatively well-paid jobs being done by women and children at a fraction of their wages. There are instances of violent demonstrations and of machines being smashed and buildings being burned but they could not stop the onrush of the industrial revolution.

Below
Arkwright's 'Spinning Jenny'

Jeremiah Ambler was typical of the many enterprising men who entered the manufacture of worsted fabric. He was originally a sheep breeder and hence would have been familiar with the trade. He started manufacturing in a disused barn with two sets of hand combs, one spinning frame, one yarn winder and half a dozen hand looms. The various processes needed to manufacture the cloth were slowly being brought under one roof, presaging the factory system of the nineteenth century.

It was by no means certain that Bradford would take a full part in the industrialisation process. Halifax and Leeds were better placed and Bradford could well have been left behind. The increased volume of trade in cloth, coal and limestone put increasing pressure on the road network then used by the packhorses to transport goods and raw materials. Groups of individuals banded together to build turnpike roads, where tolls could be charged for the use of the roads. The first of these in Bradford was opened in 1734 linking Manchester to Bradford and Leeds and the increasing network of new roads meant that stage coaches could run between Bradford and the rest of the country. Although the turnpikes improved the quality of the roads, they did not reduce the journey time of the packhorses or bring down transport costs.

Below
Stage coaches ran on the new turnpike roads

It was the opening of the Leeds to Liverpool canal which was largely to overcome these problems. The canal was a Bradford scheme from its conception in 1765 by John Stanhope to its completion in 1816. Bradford supplied many of the members of the committee which saw the project through and much of the capital needed to finance it came from Bradford colliery and land owners. Bradford was linked to the main canal in 1774 with the construction of the Bradford Canal. Now its goods could be quickly and cheaply transported to the internal markets and to the growing export trade via the ports of the Humber and the Mersey. The canal lasted until 1922 when the last cargo barge left Bradford carrying coal and it was finally dismantled in March 1995, the victim of the railways and improved roads. Despite its economic advantages, the canal had been an environmental disaster, causing both water shortages and floods and becoming so polluted with sulphur fumes that it actually caught fire in 1845 when a light fell off one of the boats using it at the time.

Right
The canal came into the centre of Bradford

The introduction of steam power, following Watt's invention of the steam engine in 1788, would be the key to Bradford's future growth. An attempt to open a spinning mill powered by steam in 1793 was frustrated by a violent demonstration of spinners and weavers who feared for their livelihoods. Bradford continued to use hand, horse and water as a source of power until 1798 when the first steam power mill started working with a fifteen horse power engine. The tide could not be stopped, despite further rioting. By 1800 some 1,290 people in Bradford out of a total population of 13,000 were employed in the manufacture of worsted, but cloth making was not Bradford's only manufacturing process. An iron works had been established at Bowling in 1778 and several collieries were being worked in the neighbourhood.

Below
Watt's steam engines powered the new mills

Bradford's middle classes were relatively few. Only 188 people are listed in the first Bradford Directory of 1792, amongst them seven 'gentry', six lawyers and six innkeepers but no mention of anyone working in the cloth industry.

John Hustler

John Hustler was one of many entrepreneurs working in Bradford in the eighteenth century but the breadth of his achievements is remarkable. He was born in 1715 into one of Bradford's influential Quaker families and went into the family business making woollen cloth. Much of his early life must have been spent in the saddle, travelling as far as Lincolnshire to buy wool and bringing it back to Bradford to be made into cloth using his own family and a number of outworkers as the labour supply. Hustler would then take the finished cloth into Bradford to sell it to one of the merchants who met at the White Lion Inn in Kirkgate. Hustler was the driving force behind many of the improvements made in Bradford in the 18th Century. In 1773 he saw the opening of Bradford's Piece Hall where merchants and cloth makers could meet to do business and for twenty-five years he was the chief proponent for the building of the Leeds to Liverpool canal with its link to Bradford. He proposed many improvements to Bradford's road network. He did not marry until he was forty-eight but raised six children and died at the age of seventy-five a much respected man.

BRADFORD IN THE NINETEENTH CENTURY

The nineteenth century in Bradford can be seen as two distinct periods. Up to 1847, free trade and rampant industrialisation were the dominant forces. Rapid growth in population and commercial activity were paid for by the human misery caused by the resultant conditions. After 1847, the town began to reform itself with the tempering of the unchecked exploitation of the environment and the work force and a gradual improvement in the quality of life for its citizens.

The new century did not begin well for Bradford. There was a disastrous flood in 1795 and the continuing wars with France meant the disruption of trade and acute distress for the working population with the doubling of food prices. The wars did give rise to the unusual trade in artificial limbs begun by Thomas and John Mann in Bradford in 1800. This prospered until well into the nineteenth century after the ending of the Napoleonic Wars with the victory at Waterloo in 1815.

New firms involved in the manufacture of worsted were opening at frequent intervals. Ramsbottom, Swaine and Murgatroyd started in 1801. John Rand was employing 240 people in his Horton Lane mill and others quickly followed. The old 'putting out' system did not disappear overnight but existed side by side with the mills until well into the nineteenth century. There were as many as 1,117 handloom weavers as late as 1851. By 1874 there were 520 worsted factories in Bradford and this increased to 746 by 1904. Bradford had become so associated with the manufacture of worsted cloth that it became popularly known as 'Worstedopolis'.

Right
A Victorian engraving of Bradford's factories

There was no 'local authority' in the modern sense or laws able to enforce standards of safety, hygiene or the age at which 'hands' were employed in the new mills. As a result, children as young as five were employed, working as long as their parents while the machines clattered. Thirteen hours a day was considered the norm. 'Where there was muck, there was money' and there was both in abundance. Coal was used to fire the new engines which drove the machines and was burned in every home. As a result, the air was choked with soot and ashes and the buildings quickly turned black. With no adequate local authority there was no sewage system, no street lighting, no police, no enforcement of housing standards, no schools and no clean water. Bradford simply spread out from its historic base around the Beck with new factories surrounded by streets of overcrowded and unsanitary 'back to back' houses. The town has been likened to a wild west town without a sheriff. Bradford was a town of glittering wealth and harrowing poverty.

Left
Children were employed in the factories besides their parents

Not every industrialist exploited his workers. Titus Salt is the best know example of an employer who attempted to make his Saltaire Works resemble a rural community with schools, workers' cottages and a range of public buildings. Yet even here the hours were long by modern standards and the work monotonous.

The new mills required thousands of workers and they came not only from the surrounding countryside but from Ireland and Europe, drawn by the hope of high wages. In 1801 the population was 13,264. By 1831 it was 43,527 and by 1901 it had reached 279,767. Bradford was the boom town of the Industrial Revolution and large fortunes were being made.

Yet all this economic growth and prosperity for some was bought at a high cost. Even the most ardent exponent of free trade was convinced that something must be done to make life tolerable for the masses if only to stop political activists and the spread of disease from the poorer sections of the town. Working men resented the strict discipline of the factory. Many of them were used to setting their own hours and taking time off when they liked and a harsh system of fines for the workers and corporal punishment for children was introduced to control working practices. This discipline, long hours and minimum wages combined with the constant threat of unemployment as new machines were introduced politicised many of the working classes. At first, this took the form of smashing the detested machinery and several lives were lost when Horsfall's Mill was attacked in 1826. The previous year, weavers and combers had organised a six month strike for improved wages and throughout the first half of the nineteenth century Bradford's workers supported the various political movements dedicated to the improvement of the lot of working people. Parliamentary reform in 1832 had brought the middle classes into the political system and the Chartist movement from 1835 intended the same for working people and was eagerly taken up by Bradford's workers.

The parish was the nominal local authority with some powers, especially over the support of the poor but it was wholly inadequate to deal with the new conditions. As early as 1803 a group of concerned townsmen, led by Edmund Peckover and Samuel Hailstone, had petitioned Parliament for an Improvement Act to enable them to provide some basic necessities such as footpaths, a water cart, a fire engine, a refuse cart and night watchmen. The town did not get any effective street lights until 1822 when gas was introduced and despite the efforts of the Improvement Commissioners the town remained filthy with refuse freely tipped into the Beck and butchers' offal and other trade waste thrown into the streets. Not surprisingly epidemics were rife with 420 dying of cholera in 1849 alone.

The National Government had stepped in and passed a number of laws designed to alleviate the worst abuses of the factory system. The 1833 Factory Act forbad the employment of children under the age of thirteen and limited the number of hours to be worked to forty-eight. A steady stream of regulations followed controlling conditions in the mines and factories. Some of the laws were ignored and not until a regular system of inspectors, with powers to prosecute, was in place did the conditions of work universally improve.

A visitor to Bradford in 1844 reported, 'Few of the streets are paved at all … pools of slop water and filth are visible all over the surface. The dung heaps are found in several places in the street and open privies are seen in many directions… Taking the general condition of Bradford, I am obliged to pronounce it to be the most filthy town I visited.' This may be a harsh judgement on Bradford as reports from many of the other newly industrialised towns paint a similar picture but the scale and speed of the change in Bradford was most pronounced.

Above
A Bradford Policeman from the 1880s

It was the 1847 Corporation Act, which saw the beginning of the slow improvement of the living and working conditions of the majority of Bradford's citizens. The Act enabled a group of Bradford's leading men to tackle some of the worst problems. A Corporation consisting of a mayor, fourteen aldermen and forty-two councillors was elected. In 1848 they introduced a police force tasked with bringing law and order to Bradford's unruly streets. They had an unenviable task and one of the new officers was beaten senseless, stripped naked and paraded round the town. But gradually, some kind of order was restored by the Corporation.

Other improvements followed, the most important for public health and comfort being a drainage system which allowed the introduction of flush toilets combined with sewage treatment works at Frizinghall and piped drinking water to domestic houses when the Corporation bought the privately owned water company which had been piping water into the homes of those who could afford it since 1744. Supplies of water were never plentiful in Bradford and the problem was only alleviated when the Corporation arranged supplies from the River Nidd over forty miles away and finally solved with the opening of the Scar House reservoir in the twentieth century. There was an attempt to regulate new working class houses but it would be many years before the worst of the slums were cleared and much nineteenth century housing stock remains in use today. There were other improvements to Bradford during the 19th century. In 1843 an infirmary was built in Westgate and in 1853 St George's Hall was opened by the mayor, Samuel Smith, as a cultural centre for concerts and public meetings. The corporation purchased Peel Park in 1870 and gave working people a place to stroll and listen to music on their precious days off. The first public library in Bradford opened in 1872.

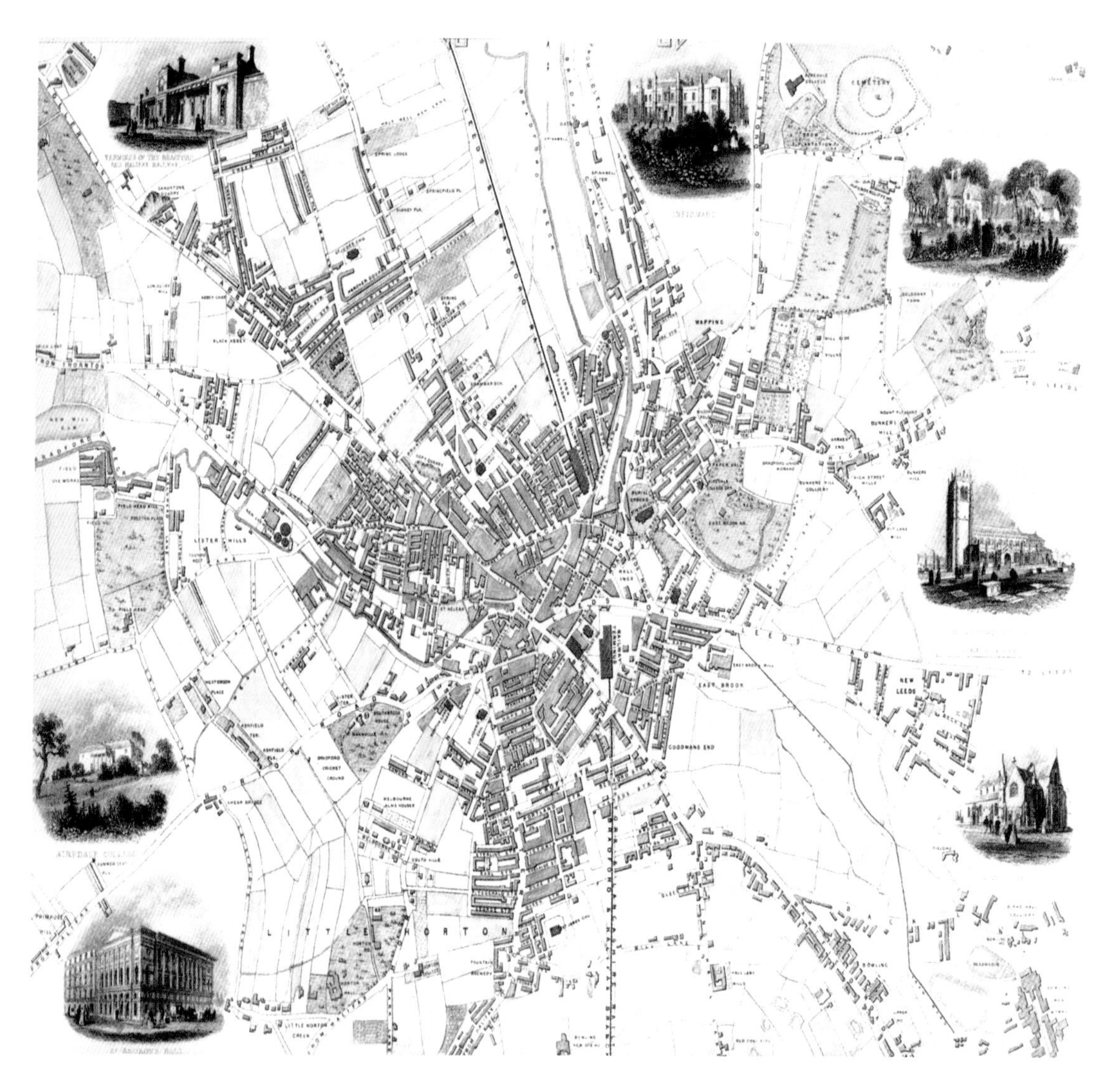

Above Bradford 1851

Above
The corner of Ivegate & Kirkgate

Right
Bradford's Town Hall was opened in1873

The most important public buildings to be built in nineteenth century Bradford were the Wool Exchange which was opened in 1864 and the grandiose Gothic Town Hall which was opened with much ceremony and civic pride in 1873 by Mayor Thompson.

Above
Trams gave way to Trolley Buses in 1909

The rapidly expanding town saw workers' houses clustered around the factories but the middle classes moved out to the more salubrious suburbs of Manningham, Little Horton and Heaton and there was a need for a public transport system to get people to work and into the city centre for shopping and leisure. In 1882 the first horse drawn trams ran in the streets but in 1889 an electric generating station was opened for domestic use and there was a sufficient supply by 1889 to allow the setting up of an electric tram system which spread out from the city centre to the suburbs. The trams gave way to trolley buses (the first in the country, beating Leeds by a few hours) in 1909 and they stayed in operation until 1972.

Although the canal and the gradually improving road system had alleviated the worst of Bradford's transport problems, the coming of the railway to Bradford in 1846 gave Bradford's manufacturers an alternative means of transporting their goods they were quick to make use of. However, the coming of the railway to Bradford was only a partial success, bedevilled as it was by the town's difficult geographic position, the rivalry of competing railway companies and the swings in trade which made the vast amount of capital required for many of the schemes difficult to organise.

By 1840 the Manchester to Leeds railway stopped at Brighouse Station and passengers for Bradford were obliged to change here and make their way the seven miles to Bradford as best they could. Plans by the Leeds & Bradford Railway Company, the Manchester & Leeds Company, the West Yorkshire Company and the Leeds & West Riding Company to build a direct line to Bradford failed to get through Parliament and only when the Manchester & Leeds Company amalgamated with the Leeds & Bradford were plans approved and the Leeds & Bradford Railway opened on the 1st of July 1846 with trains being cheered in to Bradford station. Eventually four railway companies would serve the town from their various terminals.

Above
The Midland Station at Forster Square at the end of the 19th century

But Bradford was still only a station on a spur line from Leeds and no through trains passed through Bradford to London or Edinburgh. This was felt as an affront to civic pride and the years to the end of the century were ones of continuous plans by the various companies to build vast viaducts and tunnels and whole areas of the town's centre were left waste and undeveloped as one after another of the schemes were floated and failed. The Midland Railway took up the project and progress was made in providing a direct line through the West Riding. Bradford Town Council offered an inducement of an £8000 per year rate rebate for twenty years if Bradford was joined to the line. However, by 1919 the Midland Railway finally abandoned the Bradford Through Lines plan and Bradford Corporation bought up all the property in the central area which had been acquired for demolition for £295,000. Passengers from Bradford to all areas of the country continued to 'change here'.

Although Bradford had a Grammar School as early as 1548 and it had moved into new buildings in 1873, the general provision of education for the poor of Bradford remained inadequate until the Education reforms of 1870. In 1835 of the 1,224 people married in the parish church, three-quarters of them could not sign their names. There was private education for those who could afford it but the majority of Bradford's children relied on the Sunday Schools and day schools provided by the various churches for a rudimentary education. Few children went on to any kind of secondary schooling, indeed a high proportion of pupils had finished any kind of schooling by the time they were nine. It was Forster's Education Act of 1870, which allowed the setting up of local School Boards to provide elementary schools, financed from the rates, where none were provided by the voluntary sector. Eight new schools were built attended by 24,000 children and provision for school meals, milk, health inspections and baths were introduced by the Bradford School Board which was led by Margaret McMillan. Many of the findings of the new School Health Service shocked Bradford's middle classes. Over a hundred children had not had their clothes off for more than six months and their clothes had to be burned and the children fumigated before new clothes were provided.

Below
Few children went to school in the 19th Century

Although secondary education for all would have to wait until the next century, the Bradford School Board had six secondary schools in operation by the end of the century and it was therefore possible, if rare, for a talented pupil to go all the way through to University. The need for further training in the growingly complex cloth industry led to the opening, encouraged by Forster, of a Technical College which moved into its own premises in 1882 in Great Horton Road and was opened by the Prince and Princess of Wales.

Fifty years after the setting up of Bradford Corporation, the Council petitioned Queen Victoria to grant the town city status in 1897 and this was approved. The city expanded its control taking in Allerton, Idle and Eccleshill and other areas, an expansion which would continue until 1930 when Clayton was absorbed. Continuing improvements were made by the new City Council in such matters as the provision of parks, public cemeteries, public transport and refuse disposal.

Bradford at the end of the nineteenth century had faced many of the problems thrown up by its rapid and largely uncontrolled industrialisation. Living conditions for working people had improved and better wages, shorter hours and more holidays gave rise to music halls, theatres and organised professional sports such as Bradford Rugby Football Club which started in 1866 and hobbies such as cycling, which was hugely popular with women. The losers were the churches, which saw the gradual decline in worshippers, a trend which continued into the next century and the Liberal Party which saw it working class members transfer their allegiance to the new Independent Labour Party. Ben Tillett was elected as the MP for Bradford West in 1892 and the ILP held its first national congress in Bradford the following year.

W E Forster

William Edward Forster was born in Dorset in 1819 but moved to Bradford and set up business in the wool trade in 1841. He became the Liberal MP for Bradford in 1861. He is chiefly remembered for the 1870 Elementary Education Act which gave a basic education to all the nation's children but his main work was to come later when he was chief secretary for Ireland and wrestled with the problem of Irish independence. He died in London in 1886. A statue was erected to him in 1890 in Forster Square, Bradford. The statue was taken down in 1962 when the square was redeveloped and could well have been forgotten but for the active canvassing of concerned citizens such as Horace Hird who successfully campaigned to have Forster returned to his Square in 1967.

BRADFORD IN THE TWENTIETH CENTURY

A new century was followed by a new monarch. Victoria died in 1901 to be succeeded by her son Edward VII. Many historians see the Edwardian period as a golden age of peace and prosperity at home and expansion overseas with Britain dominant in the worlds of trade and naval might. All this was to be rudely shattered by the horrors of the First World War.

Below
Horton Lane in 1904

Bradford at the beginning of the twentieth century shared in this optimism. Trade in worsted cloth had improved after the comparative slump at the end of the nineteenth century and improvements to the town's water supply and sanitation continued. In 1904 the city put on its best colours for the arrival of the Prince and Princess of Wales. They were here to unveil a statue of Queen Victoria in Little Horton Lane and to open the Bradford Exhibition at Cartwright Hall. The exhibition was meant to show off Bradford's wares but was given a popular touch with rides and exhibitions including a Somali village. Unfortunately, many of the Somali villagers died of influenza during their stay.

Left
Members of the Bradford Wool Exchange in 1905

J B Priestley gives a vivid description of Bradford before the war, which is worth quoting in full:

The Bradford I knew so well then satisfied me – no delighted me – because it was so comparatively small and compact ... I can remember walking clean across Bradford and back one Sunday evening just to catch a glimpse of a girl at a Methodist chapel service ... consider what Bradford had to offer us – three daily papers and a weekly; the Subscription concerts on Fridays, the Bradford Permanent series on Saturdays, and superb choral singing almost any night; two theatres, two music halls, two or three professional concert parties; an Arts Club; a Playgoers Society; one football club that had won the F A Cup not long before [1911]; several fine old pubs from the *George* in Market Street to the *Spotted House*, easily reached from the band concerts in Lister Park.

This may be an idealised memory, enhanced by the tragedy of the First World War. As in the rest of the country, Bradford was euphoric when war was declared against Germany in 1914 and young men clamoured at the Belle Vue Barracks to be enlisted. The reality dawned on a shocked city when the regiments known as the 'Bradford Pals' were decimated on the Somme with 515 of the 770 men who went 'over the top' with the 16th Battalion of the Prince of Wales Own West Yorkshire Regiment killed and the 18th Battalion suffering similarly casualties when it attacked.

Left
Bradford suffered heavy casualties in the First World War

Bradford's factories were at full production, making uniforms and blankets and employing increasing numbers of women in armaments factories and in jobs such as conductresses, usually done by men. Tragedy again struck the town when the Low Moor Munitions Company factory caught fire in suspicious circumstances and then exploded killing 39 people and causing damage throughout the city.

The end of the War in 1918 saw a brief boom in the demand for worsted cloth as the mills switched back to civilian manufacture but then followed almost twenty years of slump and depression with thousands out of work and some 400 textile firms closing as the pattern of world trade altered to Bradford's detriment. The city had become over-dependent on cloth manufacture and although there had been some diversification in the city's economy with the establishment of Grattans mail order business and some light engineering firms, principally Hepworth and Grandage which employed 4,000 men at its height, it was not enough to absorb the thousands of unemployed mill workers. Production did not recover until the Government abandoned free trade and imposed a 50 per cent import duty on imported cloth in 1931. Bradford's mill owners were slow to invest in the new man-made materials such as rayon, preferring to stick to what they knew best and it was not until 1937 that Courtaulds opened a rayon mill in the city. The outbreak of the Second World War in 1939 again increased demand for cloth for the armed forces and full production ensued.

The abandonment of free trade by the central government in 1931 was the culmination of the demise of Liberalism in the country. The Liberal Party itself was largely replaced by the Labour Party which took all four of Bradford's Parliamentary seats in 1945 and had a majority on the City Council. Instead of relying on market forces tempered by Christian charity, the public came to expect direct action by the Council to improve their lives and working people no longer relied on kindly employers to look after their interests but followed the traditions of Bradford's radicals and formed themselves into Unions willing to take on the employers to improve their wages and conditions of work.

The employers' answer to the inter-war depression was to cut wages and this was resisted by the National Association of Unions in the textile Trade which had formed as a single Union in 1917. In 1925 the workers were locked out for refusing the pay cuts but a public enquiry upheld their case and the pay cuts were restored. When the Trades Union Congress declared a General Strike in 1926 Bradford's railwaymen, printers and tram operatives came out and were solidly supported financially be the textile workers. Unlike in many other northern towns, the strike passed off peacefully in Bradford when the call to return to work came.

Bradford Council was active in ensuring the water supply, spending millions of pounds of rate payers' money in constructing new dams and sewage systems to take away domestic and industrial waste. It provided public transport, at first with trams and then trolley buses and motor buses. The 41 million passengers carried in 1903 had become over 126 million by 1961. With Leeds City Council it built a small aerodrome in 1930 which was to become Leeds Bradford airport after the war. It continued the work of clearing the worst of the Victorian working class housing which had disfigured the town and by 1939 had built 10,000 houses to the best standards of the day. This policy continued after the war with houses built on suburban estates such as Thorpe Edge and Bierley. Bradford Royal Infirmary opened in 1936 to supplement the many specialist medical services which had been established. Smoke free zones and the growing popularity of electricity and gas for heating did much to clean up Bradford's air.

Although the Council was run by Conservatives between the wars, the Labour councillors were active in promoting the expansion of education in the city. The aim was to provide free secondary education to the age of sixteen for all but cuts in central Government funding and the shortfall in the money available from the rates because of the depression meant that the plans were put on hold so that only a third of Bradford's children received any kind of secondary education and only a quarter of working class children who were offered places could take them up because their parents needed the wage they could bring in. Free secondary education for all had to wait until the 1944 Education Act and a Labour Government.

Above
Two fourteen year old winders at salt's Mills in the 1930s

Life for the unemployed was hard in the 1920s and 1930s but for those in work, living standards gradually improved. Bradford's growing middle classes, employed as civil servants, teachers and in the retail and banking sectors, saw the buying power of their salaries increase as prices fell and many of them could afford to buy their own homes, a small car and electrical appliances. Foreign holidays were still a luxury for the few. Shorter working hours and money to spend for some meant a growth in leisure and entertainment activities. Bradford now had two professional football clubs, Bradford City and Bradford Park Avenue and 30,000 spectators watched the game when the two clubs met in 1914. Equally successful was the city's Rugby League club, Bradford Northern, who lifted the Challenge Cup at Wembley in 1947 in front of 78,000 spectators.

The most popular form of entertainment was the cinema and Bradford had 42 picture houses by 1939. There was the Alhambra Theatre for the middle classes in Morley Street which was built in 1914 and refurbished in 1986. Along with the radio and the national newspapers, the cinema broadened people's outlooks and raised their aspirations in the same way that television was to do after the war. Traditional forms of entertainment continued with brass bands, choral unions and the public house and amateur dramatics being the most popular. In 1931 the city staged the Bradford History Pageant in Peel Park under the direction of Frank Lascelles. Some twenty-four thousand people were involved in telling Bradford's history and in displays of music and gymnastics. Despite its growth in size, on occasions such as this, Bradford could still pull together as a community and this community spirit was to be needed as the city and the country faced a second war with Germany in 1939.

The mistakes over recruitment made in the First World War were not repeated and Bradford's loss of life was comparatively light. There were few air raids and little damage to the fabric of the town although Lingard's city centre department store was destroyed in a raid on the 31st of August, 1940 in which one hundred people were injured.

The city's mills switched to war production making woollen cloth for military uniforms. There was full employment and high wages as labour became scarce but production reached such a level that there was enough spare capacity to supply the civilian markets and even export to the USA. Bradford's woollen trade was controlled by the Government's Wool Control Board which organised and rationalised supply and distribution with remarkable success.

Left
The Spinning Shed at Salt's Mill in the 1940s

For the population there was the heartbreak of the evacuation of the city's children out of the danger area to rural and distant locations where they would be safe from the expected air raids. Once the initial danger had passed many children were brought home. Some had experienced a gentler way of life but for some the experience had been less than pleasant with brothers and sisters split up and the discipline of the host families harsh. Housewives learned to queue and make the most of the ration system which was accepted as fair if irksome. People's health nationally improved as nutritional bread and vegetables and a controlled diet had their effect.

Victory in 1945 was greeted with relief and a wave of patriotism but a feeling that the lessons of the war about 'fair shares for all' should not be lost and the Labour Party swept home in Bradford and nationally. Dennis Healey, later to be Chancellor of the Exchequer, returning home to Bradford felt that 'victory would sweep away the old regimes.'

This feeling of optimism about the future and the perceived need for 'planning' at all levels of life gave rise to grandiose schemes for Bradford's future. A new city engineer, Stanley Wardley, was appointed and he devised a plan which sacrificed the Victorian heart of the city to the needs of the motor car and business accommodation. Despite protests from Bradford's Victorian Society backed by J B Priestley and David Hockney, the City Council went ahead with its plans. Down came Kirkgate Market, the Swan Arcade and the Mechanics' Institute. The Court House became a car park. In their place came concrete department stores and tower blocks which were utilitarian if not beautiful. Bradford came to resemble any other northern city with the exception of York whose City Council had the foresight to resist 'progress' and preserve the historic city centre intact. As if to emphasise what was being lost, the Town Hall was renamed the City Hall in 1965 and given a much needed clean. Once flood lit, many citizens began to appreciate its architectural value and regret what had been destroyed.

Left
Cartwright Hall

Redevelopment went on into the 1970s. In 1972 work began on a transport interchange in Bridge Street once the Bowling Beck had been diverted and the ground was cleared for the new Kirkgate Market. In the suburbs, changes were made to accommodate the new roads which were to ensure Bradford took its full place in the 'motorway age.' Dudley Hill disappeared altogether while old Bowling was cut through by the new Manchester Road. Many of Bradford's older buildings also disappeared. Horton Hall and Bierley Hall were demolished but Paper Hall, which dates from 1648 has become office accommodation and Bolling Hall a museum.

The main problem for Bradford's mill owners was a shortage of labour. There were alternatives to the mill for the workers, often paying better wages and offering more secure work in more pleasant surroundings. This pushed the wage bill up and made Bradford cloth less competitive with the growing production of Indian and European rivals. To use the machinery most efficiently it was thought necessary to switch to twenty-four hour production with shift systems and this deterred many from working in the mills. The gaps were filled at first with workers from Eastern Europe but after 1955 workers were recruited from India and Pakistan in growing numbers. By 1971 there were 30,000 workers from Asia, some 10% of the city's population and by 2001 this had grown to 85,465 or 18% of the population. The newcomers not only worked in the mills but increasingly on the city's buses which were short of labour and as families joined the men, a whole substructure of Asian shops, mosques and businesses gave employment to many.

Above
Mosques became part of the Bradford skyline

After a brief period of full order books after the war, the end for many small mills came in the early fifties when the high price of raw wool and growing foreign competition meant that small firms either went out of business or were amalgamated into larger concerns. In 1950 there were 1,123 woollen and worsted mills in Bradford. By 1967 this was down to 825 and by 2008 only four remained producing specialist cloth. The Bradford Industrial Museum, opened in 1974, is a monument to an industry, which had sustained Bradford for two hundred years. Most of the old mills have been demolished or have been used for other purposes such as Sir Titus Salt's Saltaire Mills which was declared a world heritage site and opened in 1987 by Jonathan Silver as an art gallery, featuring the work of Bradford's David Hockney, shops and restaurants.

Fortunately for Bradford, other industries were able to take the place of the declining mills. Although Jowett cars, which had begun in Bradford in 1910, ceased production in 1954 other firms making such items as tractors and televisions flourished and the 1950s and 1960s were a boom time for Bradford. Bradford University opened in 1967 with Prime Minister Harold Wilson as its Chancellor. The University had grown out of the Institute of Technology and now has 10,000 students who come from all over the UK and the world and does much for the economy and cultural life of the city. As if to remind the city of its place in the natural world, on July 2nd in 1968 torrential hail and rain hit Bradford. The flood waters swept into the city centre which turned into a lake but fortunately no one was killed.

Below
Jowett Kestrel Saloon 1935

1974 is a key year in the history of the City. Central Government began a major shake up of local government meant to bring local boundaries in line with shifts in population and economic patterns. New counties such as Avon and South Yorkshire were created and old ones such as East Yorkshire disappeared. Bradford was merged with nine other townships to form District 6A in the West Yorkshire Metropolitan County Area. Overnight, Bradford had expanded from a population of 293,000 to 462,000. 31 wards sent three councillors each, mainly Conservative, to Bradford City Hall. Old rivals from Keighley and Ilkley found themselves sitting next to each other on committees to run education, public services, housing, social services planning and management.

The new District Council was beset with problems from the start. It was run by the Conservatives until 1980 but the 1970s was a decade of industrial discontent and relative decline for Bradford. In 1978 alone, public sector workers led by the West Yorkshire Fire Service began a series of strikes while in the same year Thorn Electric made 2,000 workers redundant and more than 3,000 of Bradford's textile workers were laid off. By 1980, when the Labour Party took power at City Hall, Bradford had more than 30,000 unemployed and this rose to 37,000 in 1985. There was some good news in 1989 when Grattan's opened its 65 million pound warehouse. The Labour group held power throughout the 1990s but had no more success than its predecessors in promoting Bradford as a place to do business. The problem was seen to be one of 'image' and consultants were hired at great expense to suggest schemes such as 'Bradford's Bouncing Back' to improve this image and attract businesses to move to the city. Modernisation of the city centre continued. Woolworth's closed its store in Darley Street in 1984; the historic Theatre Royal in Manningham Lane was demolished in 1989 and Philip Smith's pie shop in Ivegate closed after 240 years of being in business. The Wool Exchange was refurbished and opened as a shopping centre in 1996. What the developers could not do, fire could and the St John Street Market, Debenham's and Eastbrook Hall were all gutted by fire.

Bradford's most tragic fire occurred on May 11th 1985. During the home match at Bradford City Football Club's Valley Parade Ground, celebrations of the Club's promotion to the second division were cut short when a fire started in the main wooden stand. The fire swept through the old structure killing 56 spectators and injuring hundreds more. The inquiry into the fire concluded that the fire was started by a discarded cigarette igniting rubbish which had accumulated under the stand.

Bradford City recovered from this tragedy to gain promotion to the top flight of English football when they were promoted to the Premier League in 1999 where they stayed for two seasons before descending back down the league tables. A remarkable recovery when it is remembered that the Club was wound up in 1983 with debts of £374,000 and was only saved by the fans who raised £43,000.

Below
Bradford City Promotion side of 1999

Above
Neil Summers heads for the line in Bradford Northern's 1993-1994 season

The successful Bradford Northern Rugby League team appeared in successive cup finals between 1947 and 1949 and played in front of 102,569 spectators at the Odsal Stadium in a cup final replay in 1954. The club was transformed into the Bradford Bulls in 1997 when Rugby League turned itself into a summer game with two divisions and promptly won the Superleague title and then in the year 2000 beat the Leeds Rhinos 24 to 18 to lift the Challenge Cup. They repeated the victory again in 2003 beating Leeds 22 to 20.

Ken Morrison retired in 2008

Although football and rugby dominated the sporting scene in Bradford, the city had more than its share of success in other sporting fields at both the national and international level. Adrian Moorhouse won gold for the 100 metres breaststroke at the 1988 Seoul Olympics. The cyclist Yvonne McGregor won a bronze medal at the 2000 Sydney Olympic Games and Junior Witter took the British light-welterweight title in boxing in 2002.

The Thatcher Government's ideology of privatisation and shifting control to the central government saw more powers taken away from City Hall be they housing or water and those successes seen in Bradford were largely those inspired by individuals such as Hockney and Silver or the Morrison family who began trading from a market store in Bradford market in 1899, and opened the first supermarket in Bradford in 1961. By 2008, the year Sir Ken Morrison retired, Morrison's was the UK's fourth largest supermarket chain. However, the Council was successful in winning large European Union development grants for the city. Slowly, Bradford was beginning to establish a reputation as a centre for culture. The refurbished Alhambra was the showpiece theatre but there were other equally successful venues such as the Priestley Centre and the Theatre-in-the Mill at the University. The amateur scene in Bradford is one of the most lively in the country ranging from the Bradford Players to the Heaton Operatic and Dramatic Society. In June 1983 the National Museum of Photography, Film and Television (since renamed the National Photo Museum) opened its doors with Britain's first IMAX cinema screen.

Yet for all these successes, the image of Bradford was badly tarnished in 1995 and again in 2001 when Muslim youths rioted and left trails of damage costing millions of pounds and causing hundreds of injuries, largely to the police force.

Above
Police and Asian gangs clash in riots that hit Bradford

There had been tensions building for some years. As early as 1984, Ray Honeyford, a local headmaster published an article in which he suggested that Bradford's Asian population would be disadvantaged in the job market if they did not learn English and understand English society better. This was seen by many as racist and he was forced to resign. Bradford's Asian community had largely congregated in the city's central area and had developed their own tightly knit communities with their own dress codes, shops, mosques and schools with little contact with their white neighbours and often very little English spoken. A policy of integration had given way to that of multi-culturalism with each community going its own way.

Below
Bradford's Asian population lived in its own tight community

Bradford Cathedral.
A call for understanding went out from all moderate church leaders

But the different cultures began to rub against each other as misunderstandings became flash points. In 1983 halal meat was served for school dinners following street demonstrations. White liberal culture could not comprehend a death threat to the author Salman Rushdie for what he had written about Islam in his book 'Satanic Verses' and growing evidence of arranged and even forced marriages in the Asian community disturbed many civil rights workers. Yet the causes of the riots remain unclear. Poor job prospects and even drug wars have been suggested. Certainly, many Asian young men felt alienated from main stream British society. Unlike their parents, they had been born in Britain yet were still seen and treated as outsiders. The gentle religion of Islam had been hijacked by small groups of extremists who preached war and death to infidels. For a small minority, religion became more important than obedience to the law or the sanctity of life itself. On September 11th 2001 Islamic extremists killed thousands of civilians in New York when they flew aeroplanes into public buildings and in July 2005, four young men from Leeds killed 52 people in London with their suicide bombs. Religious and political leaders from all sides condemned these actions and called for peace and understanding.

Bradford remains a vibrant place with much to attract the visitor and prospective businesses. With tolerance for different views and ways of life and respect for the law by all, Bradford is well placed to take its place at the forefront as one of the north's leading cities.

Bradford's multicultural community can be one of its strengths

The City Hall has become the focus of Bradford's regenerated centre

John Boynton Priestley

John Boynton Priestley was born in Bradford in 1894 and was educated there and at Cambridge. He gained national fame as a critic and broadcaster and with his first novel, 'The Good Companions' which was published in 1929 and was followed by many others. He was also a popular playwright with plays such as 'An Inspector Calls' and the comedy 'When We Are Married' which was set in Bradford and takes a fond look at the city's local politicians. He was active in politics and protest movements. He died in 1984.

Acknowledgements

The Blackthorn Press acknowledges and thanks the following for their kind assistance in providing photographs and drawings: Roy Burrell, Bradford City Museums, George Morrow, Museo Thyssen-Bornemisza.

The Blackthorn Press has attempted to contact copyright owners of artwork reproduced in this book and it welcomes queries from those not acknowledged above. Queries should be sent to Blackthorn Press, Blackthorn House, Middleton Rd, Pickering YO18 8AL.